The Taffeta Parable

The Taffeta Parable

Poems by

Laura Ingram

Cover design by Shay Culligan

ISBN: 978-1-63980-360-6

Kelsay Books
502 South 1040 East, A-119
American Fork, Utah 84003
Kelsaybooks.com

To Sam,
Because I lived.

Contents

Heaven's Hat Rack

I.

Dropping my pennies every Sunday into the offering plate,
I know better than to ask my grandmother
with her pleather purse
clutched close on her lap
if God ever gives anything back.
God, maybe a neighbor with the big black dog,
God, maybe a hitchhiker with axle grease under his thumbnail
waiting for a way home—
God could be anyone I didn't know.
God could show up at my door in the middle of the night
asking for gasoline
and I'd give it to him, with a dixie cup of coffee, too.
I would not be afraid in my nightgown,
threadbare as a bad dream.
I would kneel on the hardwood, as if in prayer
for hours afterward.

II.

I'd like to think that you took the bus
to Heaven, that you got to carry
your suitcase of moonrock and champagne bubbles
with you for the ride.
You, given a duffel bag and a body to empty and fill,
to fold every sunset you ever saw into,
so many blues you had to sit on top of it zip it up.
I hope there were billboards advertising eight-eyed angels
And I hope when you got there, someone
took your coat, showed you the hat rack, asked if you'd like to
sit down somewhere while dinner's still in the oven.

III.

I still know better than to ask my mother
if God ever gives anything back,
but every day I wish you'd let yourself in with the spare key
I leave it under the mat, obvious, in case you come home.
I don't care if you possess the paintings on the walls on your way,
if you come in through the pipes,
the cat flap, or the mailbox.
I don't care if you flicker the lights for fun,
or make the milk go bad.
You won't scare me, I promise.
Someday, I'm sure you'll appear beside me in the mirror,
both of us
with bedhead. We will brush our teeth together,
and I will know you whether
your body or not.
I will say good morning again.

The Physics of Skipping Stones

Grief takes the stairs two at a time
rocks in the pockets of her raincoat,
bright pink and borrowed from love,

unsure if the next step leads to the river or the road
Flash flood warnings sounding over someone's second-favorite
     song
Car headlights diadems in the summer haze,
in this royal procession from parking lot to drug store to stop sign
I coronate a Camry, brassy and brave as Diana with its tchotchkes
tumbling from side of side of the dashboard,
No navigator on, with a wet dog hanging from the window, this is
     the Princess, bulimic and bewildered
I carry it all in my rucksack, because I, like anyone, have a bag and
     a body to carry it all, still a student, books and browned bottles
     and broken teeth.

I take the stairs two at a time, just as my grandfather taught me,
     just
as my grandfather did before he died.
Because time is just at the top, wearing the raincoat of love, her
     pockets turned wrong side out, all her treasures of pinecones
     and skipping stones scattered over the foyer, and I gather the
     sticks and mud and a frog and snail, stay there, so still, on my
     hands and knees.

Ring Finger Elegy

Poem as sore tooth,
poem as plague bag
poem as smelling salts, as scented sachet in the dresser drawer
poem as skinned elbow, bloody nose, broken bone,
poem as hand over heart, heart as hand over hand,
heart as hand in pocket, clasping for quarters to waste in the
    wishing well,
the heart is a hand, always gripping, white-knuckled—
sometimes I hold my own hand,
skidding home on slick streets after rainstorm
poem as hail storm, as maelstrom,
poem as countdown, poem as unlit landing strip,
poem as plane crash, poem as pilot, poem as pedestrian calling
    police
poem as witness to the wreck.

Still Life, with Carrot Shavings

Or: Self Portrait of the Anorexic in Real Time

Washing the empty bowl out with both hands,
as if giving a baby its first bath,
I cradle its pink plastic chin,
round as fire, as family,
as the carrots I have carved into coins
with a Leatherman,
although I know better than to keep something so sharp in the
    kitchen—

hunger is the pocketknife I never leave the house without
serrated side slicing me into seraphim, then
cephalophore of sorts;
I carry my head like a handbag,
pulling out the endless silk handkerchiefs of despair,
digging around loose change and crumpled receipts
that make a catalog of what I once wanted.

To grow older is mostly to have once wanted,
to only be beatified as beautiful once I have learned
to kneel, jagged knees tearing through my tights
at the base of the mausoleum,
to turn the dead into Gods—
because isn't that how we convince ourselves of heaven,
to worship the browning sinew of reluctant saints,
as if their crumbling wide mouths full of moss
could teach me not to need,
to seal myself shut for as long as a war and an uprising;
to never ask for anything.

The Solitude of the Female Preying Mantis

You stand, one foot over the other, at the crooked creek's mouth
mossy rocks erupting from the mud like sore molars—
your reflection drowns downstream
without you to watch over her.
No one walks you home.

The ceiling fan hums Chopin's opus 9 number 2
you are his heart, picked in a jar
pink and stopped as another planet,
one without water
or maybe the middle peddle on the piano

You are the taxidermied bird perched atop
encyclopedias in the museum gift shop
World Book towering over Merriam Webster—
the female preying mantis devouring
the unseeing eyes of her male mate

you clean up after the party no one showed up to
watch rainbows rise from the dishwater
knuckles deep in stinging suds.

You wake up alone to the rain on the window,
quieter than Keats
walk in your yarn socks to the kitchen for coffee,
cold hand over your yawn
to keep your satin ghost from slipping out
the stitch of it loose in your throat
because you are a woman, and a girl,
and you could cough up your ghost if you wanted to
leave it in a silky heap for some stranger to curl up
and sleep under.

Ode to Animal Sentinel

After "Wild Geese" by Mary Oliver

You do not have to be good
you can swallow the bird nestled silent
between your teeth
you began as the pit in God's stomach
cawing as the startled animal
of your becoming body

crawled through heaven's catacombs
at any shrill moment
being born as a warning.

Salem Song

Mother of field mice,
queen of chrysanthemum
dead flowers clutched in clenched fist
in this month of yellow leaves and red
sun with smoke wrapped around her shoulders
like a loose shawl

It is easy to blame the early dark, the empty cellar, especially when
witching hour comes and goes without candlelight
we are all so hungry in the market of misplaced things
famine of memory, or maybe truth

A fox scuffles the forest floor
tail tucked into a steel trap
the men mistake it for a hairy specter
lay down inert and intimate with the dawn
bring nothing back but soup bones

In the dandelion daytime, children help peddle silver spoons
practice bloodletting in case of plague,
peeling scabs off skinned elbows
singing soft between beestings
they get their fill of rainwater
and we raise them on ragweed and skipping rope rhymes
leave them dreaming alone, three to a bed.

Spinster Manifesto

Eighty-eight and you've started cutting eyeholes
in every quilt, just in case
you always knew you would be the one
stitching your own ghost.

think about where you will be buried
out back with the bird bath
toes pointed toward the hermit in her hovel;
all women, on trial or not, at least half witch.

Equinox Coda

Here in Virginia
The rain this morning falls
on the snow from last night
I walk down the dirt road, alone
my shoes make slurping sounds in the ground like
the first sip of lukewarm cherry wine at thirteen in a friend's
    basement
junior high, and the winter trees remind of girls in the locker room
naked and hunched, skinny arms crossed over their budding chests
adolescent hearts so apparent, heavy as rotting apples under their
    training bras,
grass-stained and thudding to the ground

I can smell the new grass under the snowmelt
turn towards home knowing
and I do not need to carry anything with me
for April to creep after me up the hill again.

3: Pain is very noticeable, like a bee-sting or an injection

The Tuesday after I came out of the hospital for the fourth-odd time, Notre Dame de Paris caught fire. Built before the finishing of most fairy tales, the cathedral, ancient as fever, kept safe in its catacombs several swarms of bees. Because bees lack lungs, they all survived the smoke, stilling to sleep in the hippocampus of the cathedral. Supernovae never shrink, but city spires crumble, gaseous nebulas collapse, and soft tissue catabolizes. The body, like the chapel, will be rebuilt, over and over, by the pressing of hot palms against its walls until a sanctuary with its rows of wooden seats—or a heart with its jam-packed coat-closet—flames open like a crimson flower at the tenderness of so much touch. Joan of Arc may have burned, like the building, but Saint Catherine of Sienna starved and I canonized her hunger in my childhood bedroom.

The bees in my steeple die.

Two Swallows

To H., At Sea

The early dark stands on its hind legs
to watch me undress through the curtains
sheer as dreams
while I unbutton the day I've had like a blouse,
leaving it in a floral heap on the floor
by the unmade bed.
night scampers off on all fours
I cradle the aging cat
and wonder if the sea also struggles
to sleep by itself.

The wars you go to without me
hit the news late at night—
we women and children don't want to watch.

A sailor is not a soldier, but
you climb on a ladder of wind,
water below you the blue of rot
spotting the oranges
heaped high in the mess deck, untouched
by the callused thumbs of seamen
months shy of seeing the sun.

Whether you suffer from scurvy or heartache,
the corpsmen ferry their flannel cures
and I wish to live another whole life long
as the collar on your coat,
close enough to keep the cold off your cheek.

Casual Contact

It was a neon year, '88, the year we moved into the studio on west Strauss, too far from the train station, tacky lights twice taped over the scarred headboard your sister let us have, all eighteen books I owned teetering in a stack on the floor. You swore to me you'd build them a shelf, because I always insisted books deserve the respect of their own proper place just as much as anybody else with a slumped spine and a hundred thousand words or so to say.

You started working at the hospital as an orderly in the auburn of October, not the hospital where your father died, no, but you said that didn't matter because they were all the same with their off-brand antiseptic cleansers, their instant coffee in Styrofoam cups, their waiting rooms as endless as an earthquake, with a thousand moving mouths to populate the damp of your dreams; did you know, you told me at least twice a week, kicking off your shoes and rubbing your raw toes red, that every face you see in a dream is someone you passed by in the park, sat next to on an airplane—that your brain can't create a face you've never seen, a face you have forgotten of a girl delivering a baby in an unlocked bathroom stall, trying to find a wheelchair and talk to her through her hanging hair, a face from the infomercials we always ended up falling asleep to. I pressed my chapped lips to your chapped cheek and we didn't dream.

You worked as an orderly into December, collar pulled up against the cold, coffee sloshing over the rim of your Styrofoam cup, the wind whispering its name in your ears. You worked as an orderly until you couldn't anymore, tripping over the cheap tinsel tangled still and silver as the snow, until you started waking up at night with nosebleeds. We went to the hospital together then, where we waited on hard plastic chairs, holding our own hands while magazine mothers shush bundles of blankets to sleep.

You used to work as an orderly, the nurse says with a nod when she tells us you tested positive, my nails leaving half-moons in your hand. You don't cry until it's dark out, breaking into your hands at the kitchen table, pamphlets fanned out over the oak. I make you tea and toast, as if the worst thing in the world hasn't just happened, and just like always you eat the crusts first.

We find a support group that meets, like most support groups, in a church basement full of folding chairs and discount lemonade, feel our suffering like Godliness, begging for belief, but people we don't know still shout "faggots" out their frostbitten car windows when we pass by, especially after your new pills come in, and your bushy black hair comes out by the handfuls, sores splitting your chapped lips.

We do go see my mother, who doesn't know you, even now, and I introduce you as my friend and she knows whatever she thinks you are, you are more than that, kisses your forehead unafraid. I carry you, slumped into sleep, to the car after I tell her almost everything, headlights glinting, brassy as Mardi Gras beads draped around the clouds' narrow necks, and I count them the whole way home.

We don't go see your mother, even though I ask you to call her every afternoon, sickly-thin sun pooling at our feet from the unopened window, because you are weather-cold and withering and I miss you just as much as I've ever loved you.

Pulse Point

That roll of quarters for the phone call home
that three-way mirror in a department store dressing room
silver and speckled as the premonition of prophets
dream-spangled girl, divine as David
that chipped porcelain angel rotting
in the rain amongst rhododendrons
that list of names stamped in the back of the library book
that baby bird buried by the creek bed
that funhouse, that freakshow, those twins with two heads—
that horror, that headstone,
that hole in the damp dark earth.

Girl

After "To the Woman Crying Uncontrollably in the Next Stall"
by Kim Addonizio

if you ever cut your own bangs with kiddie scissors stuffed your
    purple training bra with pink Kleenex
got asked out as a joke by a group of boys, always three, arms
    crossed over your flat chest, heart a knuckled first, pulse a knock
    on a locked door
if you ever wrote a novel in a spiral notebook
first bled in the back of algebra two, wearing a white skirt because
    of course you were, used one-ply toilet paper as a pad
stood sunburned at the edge of the ocean, seaweed clinging to your
    feet flashing quick and white as two minnows—
if your first kiss felt like biting your own tongue, unsaid, hands
    shaking like separate flurries of December snow
swam clothed in a river with no name cried until you threw up
if you ever hid a bad haircut with a worse hat had only your hands
    to cover your heart
dreamed staccato as unnumbered opus, or didn't dream, but stayed
    up to watch the sun scamper up the sky on all fours, a soft yellow
    dog
morning has come again.

Creation Myth of the Honor's Student

Fifteen

At fifteen I'd soak in the bathtub until my skin pruned purple, swaddle into a sweater, eyes shut, and pretend I had just been born, wailing at my reflection, the first thing I'd encounter. I'd stay to see me standing there, so thin, scrape the sugared pink top of my sadness with my teeth, swallow it like a wad of bubblegum, even knowing it'd be seven years before it would pass through my body, my body born as the runt in a litter of stars, my body delivered in the penumbra, doused in earthshine, conceived as a lump in the cosmos's throat.

I am my own daughter.

At fifteen my hair came out in handfuls and I hadn't had my first kiss. At fifteen girls stopped their sacred rituals of painting their eyes like evening over porcelain sinks to ask me What's Your Secret and I'd pretend to not know what they were talking about, dumping my sandwich in the wastebasket on the way out.

At fifteen I'd come home from school hungry enough to eat the yellow yolk of sun with a slice of buttered sky, go to bed thirsty for mother's milk of Andromeda, holding onto my hipbones like handrails as I descend the staircase to dreams.

The Hated Starlings

You, nestled in the moon's age-spotted breast
like a lover's locket
folded photo tucked fading into your mirrored heart
silver and exacting as the vanity glass,
or the window where the wartime wife waits
frosty breath obstructing her face.

The dressing room fluorescence eclipses
your allergy to self.
You see your reflection only in the penumbra
otherwise, you cannot bear
to witness your own wince
even when washing teaspoons.
You stare instead at the clock,
let the orbit of hours
obscure everything else.

You forget to fill the seed trough
but it won't be the first time
the hated starlings starve.
Three of them huddle at the feeder anyway.
Ducking between fenceposts,
looking for Carlos-William's red wheelbarrow
so much depends on what
you can no longer carry—
arms aching as you exhume
an injured mouse
from rotting wood
the beads of its spine too small
to hold enough prayers
to begin to be forgiven.

The third starling, a straggler
comes closer to your hand than the others
she perches on your tattooed arm
and reflected in her feathers,
you see yourself, iridescent as you always have been
rising with the rainbows off her rain-slicked wing.

August Jeremiad

Your courage is a thicket of ragweed roving by roadside
nothing but dust motes and dandelions for miles
lungs full of telephone wire—when you open your mouth, there's
the dial-tone
a goodbye that lasts until the locusts
a goodbye as loud as Lamentations

you, with a mouthful of radio static and broken molars
you, waking up from the nightmare screaming every name in the
　　old testament

from backseat to river bank
you said you didn't know how to swim
never learned to breathe in that many blues

We were granted a skipping stone as our moon
a moon to orbit and eclipse,
yank us around by our necks

we packed a picnic lunch

every day that summer
gingham skirts waving like
handkerchiefs of soldier's wives in the wind
trying to drown ourselves so solemn
walking home barefoot and sunburnt
the beehives of our brains flooded to the honeycombs.

The Winter Garden

The clouds whisper rumors to the windows,
sky snubbed, lonesome and far from the farmhouse
back turned to that friendless star, the shy sun,
hands over her head.

Early January, cleaning up my grandmother's sunroom,
I find a photo of myself, maybe seven, maybe eight,
always small for my age,
somber as Eve after Eden,
holding a paperback over my heart
hands folded inside each other like fresh socks in the drawer

it's so often said that you never forget how to ride a bike
but I lose my balance more than once on the hot-pink two-wheeler
fingers slipping through the streamers on the handlebars
brown brittle grass sticking to my skirt when I tumble.

My grandmother's name is my name,
and wheeling the bike I forgot how to ride back by the winter
    cabbage heads,
towards the porch filled with empty pots and seed packets for some
    recalcitrant spring
daydreams were a housecoat she wore to rags as a young wife.
I wonder if she ever rested her forehead on this window as I do
    today, and cried hard
for whatever she hoped would never happen.
I only want to open the door, step into the cold,
and keep walking, face turned up to soft kiss of dark.

The Heaviness of an Animal Heart

I read in the eighth grade that the average giraffe heart
weighs around twenty-five pounds,
over half of my heretic adolescent body
with its aching, treasonous chest that would not bud
and would not bud.
Walking out of the library, winter sun
arching its back like an orange cat
spring is never soon.

I imagine my heart as a spool of embroidery floss,
a basket of plums, no, one of those tiny oranges people pack
in their sack lunches at school and work,
my heart peeled with clumsy fingers.
My heart of fragrant rind and white pulp,
my heart, a tinder box, a harmonica, a carton of cigarettes—
my heart, slung over one shoulder like a hobo's sack,
My heart as whatever letter or locket I'd carry from my house on
    fire,
My heart, the coat closet, my heart,
the waiting room,
enough chairs for everyone—
come sit down.

To Everything There Is a Season

A day in ACUTE ICU for eating disorders during COVID-19

I hold my own hand in the hospital bed and it feels like my house keys, sun streaking my window with her thousand fingerprints. It is morning and while the rest of the world shuts down businesses, closes schools, and cancels church services, here at the hospital breakfast still arrives at eight thirty. I still step on the scale backwards at seven and get my IV bag replaced at five. My nurse, with eyes red and swirling as NBC night news over the mask the attending handed her on her way in this morning, it wasn't required yesterday, still tells me that food is my medicine, and when I stir my granola and yogurt with a bent spoon, I eat the shame too, thick and clotted like the cream at the top of the cup, chew and swallow and almost choke on bites of shame that I am safe.

Outside, across the cul-de-sac, where the emergency room looms, magazine mothers scurry, masked, infants loud as advertisements. Inside, trays dotted dark with Jell-o swarm the hallways while my nurse turns off the news, says I don't need to see, and I look away, I do, down from the window at the empty, decaffeinated street, and while I am sobbing over a ham sandwich on rye, sporing wildly with my plastic spork, another girl on another floor of the hospital is sobbing over a Styrofoam cup of hospital coffee while she waits for her father's test results to come back, tears soaking through her paper mask and I think about her, maybe Maria, without a last name, but dinner still ends at six thirty, same as always so I keep my eyes on the clock.

The Taffeta Parable

After "Dedication to Hunger" by Louise Glück

I.

It beings,
as anything begins
with a female child
burying her own baby teeth
in a fairy ring by the birdbath out back
always wishing for more wishes
stirring mud potion with sticks.

She reads two library books every afternoon
last late autumn light haloed over her hair
head bowed over fairytale and folklore.
Still in a swing, Mary Janes dragging through the dirt
mouthing myth on the playground
knowing the prettier girl plays the part of princess—
but the witch is the one who makes the magic, anyway.
The odd eleven-year-old girl, powerful as fable,
sitting alone in front of an untouched lunch tray.

II.

Fifteen and her first kiss feels like
she is the shimmering magician's
assistant in the vanishing
act, the ubiquitous illusion—
sawing a smiling woman in half,
the rest of her rolled backstage in a box.
The story is always the same;
women's bodies shrinking for the show,

even Eve's apple, Lilith's absence—
asceticism or ascension
girlhood or godliness—
it's all the same power of
appearances,
of taking care to remain unseen.

III.

It never ends, really
simply sours like the saucer of milk
sitting out too long—
some bluing November night
when the cross-eyed calico doesn't come home.
She cradles her loneliness close to her chest,
fans it out like a hand of cards.
Playing gin rummy with the poker-faced year
while the teakettle teaches itself to sing
she shuffles the endless deck of hunger and hearts
knowing she won't win—
neither ever runs out.

About the Author

Laura Ingram is the author of five volumes of poetry: *The Solitude of the Female Preying Mantis, The Taffeta Parable, Animal Sentinel, Mirabilis, Junior Citizen's Discount,* and *The Ghost Gospels.*

Her poetry and prose have appeared in over one-hundred journals and magazines, among them Gravel, Thuya Poetry Review, Random Sample Review, and Five on the Fifth. Laura has served as Poetry Editor for *The Blue Mountain Review.* She is an alumna of Appomattox Regional Governor's School for the Arts and Technology as well as Hollins University. Laura lives between gossamer and corrosion. She is a twenty-six-year-old relic. She resides in rural Virginia and enjoys most books and all cats.

www.ingramcontent.com/pod-product-compliance
Lightning Source LLC
Chambersburg PA
CBHW031009090426
42737CB00008B/747